WHAT MAKES A BIRD?

THE ANIMAL KINGDOM

Lynn M. Stone

The Rourke Book Co., Inc.
Vero Beach, Florida 32964

PHOTO CREDITS
All photos © Lynn M. Stone

EDITORIAL SERVICES:
Penworthy Learning Systems

Library of Congress Cataloging-in-Publication Data

Stone, Lynn M.
    What Makes a Bird? / by Lynn M. Stone.
        p. cm. — (The Animal Kingdom)
    Includes index
    Summary: Discusses the habits, bodies, and different kinds of
birds and their relationships with people.
    ISBN 1-55916-194-9
    1. Birds—Juvenile literature. [1. Birds] I. Title II. Series: Stone,
Lynn M.   Animal Kingdom.
QL676.2.S76 1997
598—dc21   96–52181
                                                           CIP
                                                           AC

Printed in the USA

TABLE OF CONTENTS

BIRDS

Birds are animals with feathers and wings. Most birds use their wings to fly. Some birds, however, cannot fly.

Birds are **vertebrate** (VER tuh BRAYT) animals because they have a backbone. Unlike most other vertebrates, such as mammals, birds do not have teeth.

Birds are **warm-blooded** (WARM BLUD ed). The bodies of warm-blooded animals keep a steady temperature in hot or cold weather. People are also warm-blooded.

Most birds have lightweight, air-filled bones that help them to fly.

Wings and air-filled, hollow bones help birds like this roseate spoonbill lift from the ground and fly.

HABITS OF BIRDS

Many birds travel over great distances because they can fly. They may nest in the north then travel south for the winter.

Their long journeys are migrations. Many birds migrate, but the Arctic tern is the champion. It travels 11,000 miles (17,700 kilometers) each way from the Arctic to the Antarctic and back.

Flying birds reach speeds over 100 miles an hour (160 kilometers). A bird diving through the air can fly even faster.

Hundreds of thousands of snow geese migrate from Canada to the southern United States each fall.

KINDS OF BIRDS

Nearly 10,000 **species** (SPEE sheez), or kinds, of birds have been discovered. Scientists believe that very few species remain to be found.

About 700 bird species live in North America north of Mexico. They range in size from tiny hummingbirds to 30-pound (thirteen and one-half kilograms) swans.

Scientists place North American birds in 21 major groups. They group birds largely by their body shape, features, and habits.

The family of hawks, eagles, and vultures is one of the best-known groups.

Colorful king vulture of Latin America is one of several kinds of birds of prey.

WHERE BIRDS LIVE

Birds live in almost every **habitat** (HAB uh TAT) on Earth. Habitats are living places, such as marshes, ponds, and prairies.

More bird species live in warm, tropical habitats than anywhere else. But several kinds of penguins and petrels live on or near Antarctica. Antarctica is the coldest place in the world.

Birds in cold places have dense feathers and a layer of fat to keep them warm.

King penguins live in groups called colonies on the icy shores of sea islands near Antarctica.

Baby swans follow their parents around, but they feed themselves.

Many birds, like the black skimmer here, nest on the ground. Their eggs are often the same color as the sand, soil, or plants.

BODIES OF BIRDS

The way a bird is built tells much about where it lives and what it eats. Each species of bird has a body that works well in its own special habitat.

A bird with webbed feet, for example, lives in a watery habitat. A bird with webbed feet and a torpedo shape dives in the water.

A long-legged bird is most likely a wader. A bird with clawed toes, or **talons** (TAL unz), and a sharp, curved beak is a hunter.

A pelican's bill is a big bucket for catching fish.

AMAZING BIRDS

Some birds have amazing habits, shapes, or features. The ostrich has a 300-pound (140 kilogram) body. Its wings are floppy and useless, but the ostrich runs like a deer.

The male prairie chicken has a balloonlike pouch on its throat for calling mates.

Cranes dance. Emperor penguins lay their eggs during the Antarctic winter. The toucan has a huge bill that looks like a banana.

Bearded vultures break open bones by dropping them during flight.

With its long, yellow beak, the keel-billed toucan in flight looks like a flying banana.

PREDATOR AND PREY

Birds eat a huge variety of plant and animal foods. Exactly what a bird eats depends upon the kind of bird—and the time of year. Some birds are true **predators** (PRED uh terz). They kill other animals, their **prey** (PRAY), so they can eat. Eagles, for example, attack fish and small land animals.

Some birds are themselves prey. Many young birds are taken from nests by bobcats, snakes, raccoons, and other hunters.

Certain **falcons** (FAL kunz) attack other birds, striking them with talons in midair.

Talons reaching out, a bald eagle grabs a fish from the sea in Alaska.

BABY BIRDS

Mother birds lay eggs, usually in a nest. The adult bird's feathers keep the eggs warm until they hatch.

Most kinds of baby birds stay in the nest for several days or weeks. The parents bring food to them.

A few baby birds, such as geese and cranes, leave the nest immediately. They stay with their parents but feed themselves.

Most young birds can fly just a few weeks after hatching.

A wood stork parent coughs up a fishy soup to feed its chick.

PEOPLE AND BIRDS

People enjoy the beauty, songs, and flight of birds. Early peoples could only imagine what it was like to fly. By studying birds' flight, people learned to build flying machines.

Birds are extremely important to people in North America. People use birds for food, sport, pets, and pleasure. Millions of North Americans enjoy watching birds.

The United States uses the bald eagle as the nation's symbol.

Many kinds of birds are rare. Some are in danger of disappearing. We can help protect birds by protecting their habitats.

Glossary

falcon (FAL kun) — a slender hawk with narrow wings for quick, twisting flight

habitat (HAB uh TAT) — the special kind of place where an animal lives, such as northern forests

predator (PRED uh ter) — an animal that hunts other animals for food

prey (PRAY) — an animal that is hunted by another animal for food

species (SPEE sheez) — within a group of closely related animals, one certain kind, such as a *trumpeter* swan

talons (TAL unz) — the toe claws of birds of prey, such as eagles

vertebrate (VER tuh BRAYT) — an animal with a backbone; a fish, amphibian, reptile, bird or mammal

warm-blooded (WARM BLUD ed) — refers to birds and mammals, animals whose bodies keep a steady, warm temperature even in cold weather

INDEX

DATE DUE

P-28 4			
11-21	22		
GAYLORD			PRINTED IN U.S.A